Beautiful Birds

Valerie Davies

Created and produced by Andromeda Children's Books
An imprint of Pinwheel Ltd
Winchester House
259–269 Old Marylebone Road
London NW1 5XJ, UK

This edition published in 2007 by School Specialty Publishing,
a member of the School Specialty Family.

School Specialty® Publishing

Library of Congress Cataloging-in-Publication Data
is on file with the publisher.

Send all inquiries to: School Specialty Publishing
8720 Orion Place
Columbus, OH 43240-2111

ISBN 0-7696-4824-X

1 2 3 4 5 6 7 8 9 10 PIN 10 09 08 07 06

Printed in China

Author: Valerie Davies
Art Editor: Gillian Shaw
Editor: Elise See Tai
American Editor: Sue Diehm
Art Director: Miranda Kennedy
Production Director: Clive Sparling
Illustrators: Rob Dyke (Bernard Thornton Artists), Robert Morton
(Bernard Thornton Artists), Gill Tomblin
Apologies for any
unintentional omissions.

Contents

Introduction

There are about 9,700 **species of birds**. They live in almost every **habitat** on earth. All birds have wings and most can fly. They have lightweight skeletons, which make it is easier to fly.

The sword-billed hummingbird has a long, thin beak.

Beaks

Birds have beaks, or **bills**, instead of teeth. The shape of the beak differs according to the type of food the bird eats. Seed-eaters have short, cone-shaped beaks that they use like nutcrackers. Woodpeckers have bills like chisels that they use to drill into trees to find insects. Owls and hawks have hooked beaks for tearing flesh.

Feathers

Birds are the only living animals that have feathers. Feathers have different purposes. Some feathers keep the body warm and others are used for flying.

Long and Short Legs

Birds that spend most of their time wading or running have long legs. Birds that spend most of their time in the air have very short legs. Birds that spend time in trees have short, strong legs that help them climb and perch.

The snowy owl's feathers help keep it warm.

Ears, Noses, and Eyes

Birds have excellent hearing and eyesight. The ear openings are covered by feathers on the sides of the head. Their senses of smell, taste, and touch are not well-developed. Their nostrils are on the top of the beak and are used for breathing, not smelling.

The male mandarin duck is very colorful.

Eggs

All birds lay eggs and hatch from eggs. Eggs differ in shape, size, and color to fit into their surroundings. Most eggs are laid in nests built by the female or her mate.

Extinct Birds

Since the 1600s, about 80 kinds of birds have died out, or become **extinct**. Human beings have contributed to this problem by overhunting or destroying their environments. In the 1800s, there were about five billion passenger pigeons in North America. They became extinct in 1914 after they were hunted for food and sport. Another well-known extinct bird is the dodo, a flightless bird. Today, more than 2,000 species are **endangered**, or at risk of extinction.

The dodo became extinct 300 years ago.

Colorful Birds

Most male birds are more colorful than female birds. The males' bright colors attract the female birds of their species. Female birds have dull-colored **plumage**, or feathers, which serve as **camouflage**. This helps them blend in with their surroundings when they are sitting on their nests.

Size

Birds vary a great deal in size. The tiny bee hummingbird is just 2 in. (5 cm) long, and the huge ostrich can grow to 8 ft. (2.4 m) tall!

Flightless Birds

Emperor Penguins

There are about 55 species of flightless birds. They developed from birds that could fly. Many flightless birds lived on islands where they had few **predators**, so they had no need to fly away to escape. Some used running and swimming instead of flying. All flightless birds are native to the southern hemisphere.

Cassowary

The wings of the **emperor penguin** have developed into flippers over millions of years. They allow the penguin to propel itself through water. This penguin lives in Antarctica. It protects itself from the cold by huddling in groups. Each male **incubates** one egg on its feet to keep the egg warm.

The 5-ft. (1.5-m) tall **cassowary** has a long spike on each foot. When threatened, it leaps feet-first at its enemy to stab it with these spikes. Like penguins, the male incubates the eggs, then cares for the chicks for up to nine months.

Kiwi

The **peacock** is native to India and Sri Lanka. Its body is very heavy and its wings are weak, but it can flutter into trees or onto rooftops to **roost** for the night. In the breeding season, the male peacock fans its colorful feathers to attract a female mate.

The **kiwi** lives in New Zealand. It has nostrils at the tip of a long beak that help it smell worms under the ground. It has no tail and tiny, useless 2-in. (5-cm) wings. It is often attacked by cats and dogs.

Flightless Cormorant

Peacocks

The **flightless cormorant** lives in the Galapagos Islands. It has few feathers on its wings, and it usually stands with its wings outstretched. Its long bill helps it to pick up octopus and fish from the sea floor. A special lens on each eye allows it to see underwater.

Ostrich

The ostrich lives in the dry grasslands and semi-arid deserts of Africa and southwestern Asia. The ostrich is the tallest, heaviest living bird in the world. Males can grow to be 9 ft. (2.7 m) and weigh 150–300 lbs. (68–136 kg). Although the ostrich does not fly, it has small, strong wings covered with drooping feathers. The ostrich flaps its wings when threatened or when it courts female ostriches.

Hiding From Danger

It is difficult for an ostrich to hide from predators because it lives in areas with little vegetation. If alarmed, a group of ostriches will tuck their heads and necks in close to their bodies, fluff out their feathers, and stand still. From a distance, they look like a group of bushes on thin stems.

Killer Legs

The ostrich's powerful legs can deliver a kick strong enough to kill a lion! Its long, powerful legs also allow it to run quickly.

Living in Groups

The ostrich lives and travels in groups. It feeds on the leaves, roots, flowers, and seeds of many plants. When feeding, the ostrich's head is so close to the ground that it cannot look out for predators, so one or two other ostriches watch for danger.

Ostrich Eggs

The male bonds with the main female but has two to six other females in its **flock**. The main female lays her eggs first. One egg is about 6 in. (15 cm) long. Each egg weighs about 3 lbs. (1.4 kg). The male sits on the eggs at night, and the main female incubates them during the day.

Long neck and good eyesight help detect predators

Looking After the Eggs

Besides keeping the eggs warm at night, the male also protects them from predators, such as jackals and hyenas.

Long, powerful legs used for defense and running

Ostrich Chicks

One week before they are due to hatch, the chicks start cheeping inside the eggs. After they hatch, the parents watch over them. If the chicks are threatened, the adults distract predators by pretending to be injured. This action lures the predators away from the chicks.

No feathers on legs

The young chick hatches fully-feathered and able to run

AMAZING FLIGHTLESS BIRD FACTS!

● The kiwi is the only survivor of an ancient group of birds that included the now-extinct moa.

● The flightless cormorant has feathers that are not completely waterproof, even though it feeds underwater.

● Ostrich chicks are half to two-thirds grown by their first year.

● The ostrich has two large toes on each foot to give it better balance when it runs.

● The ostrich does not have feathers on its legs.

● The ostrich does not bury its head in the sand, as often thought.

● The ostrich is the fastest running animal on two legs. It can reach speeds of 45 mph (72 km/h).

Colorful Birds

Parrots, hornbills, and woodpeckers are known for their large, strong beaks and colorful feathers, or plumage. There are about 740 species in this group. These birds make their nests in holes, usually in trees. Sometimes they take over old owl-nest holes.

The **kea** belongs to the parrot family. It is an unusual parrot because its feathers are a dull-colored olive green. This coloration camouflages the bird during the day. The kea is **nocturnal**, feeding at night. It has strong legs for walking and climbing, but its heavy body does not allow it to fly well.

Lorikeets

Kea

The **lorikeet** is related to parrots, and many have the same colorful plumage. It feeds mainly on **nectar** from flowers. Its tongue has a brush-like tip that the bird uses to scoop nectar into its mouth. It crushes harder fruits or seeds inside its beak to obtain their juices.

The **acorn woodpecker** uses its beak like a drill to make holes in trees. Its skull is padded so there is no damage to its head. The woodpecker stores thousands of acorns in the holes it makes in trees and telephone poles.

Acorn Woodpecker

The **aracari** has a long, curved beak with jagged edges. It uses these edges to crush fruit, insects, and even the small reptiles it eats. It lives and sleeps in small flocks, and roosts in tree cavities.

Aracari

Toco Toucan

The colorful orange bill of the **toco toucan** is about 8 in. (20 cm) long and 3 in. (8 cm) high at its base. The bird uses its bill as a tool to pick fruit from the ends of thin branches. The toucan tosses back its head to throw food from the tip of its bill into its throat.

Green-Winged Macaw

The green-winged macaw lives in the **rain forest** trees of South America. The bright-red feathers on its head and neck and the blue feathers on its tail make it a very colorful parrot. Its bright-green plumage gives excellent camouflage among the leaves and flowers. Its feet have two toes pointing forward and two toes pointing backward. These toes help it climb trees and also allow the parrot to hold food with its feet and place it in its beak.

Favorite Foods

The macaw eats fruit, seeds, and nuts. Some of the fruit is unripe or poisonous. These birds do not get sick because they eat river clay. This clay contains a mineral called *kaolin*. This mineral prevents the birds from becoming ill.

Large, strong beak for eating fruit, seeds, and nuts

Fast Fliers

Despite having a large body, the green-winged macaw can fly quickly. The narrow, pointed shape of its wings allows it to fly easily because there is little wind resistance.

Long, narrow wings for flying

Flocks

Green-winged macaws are noisy birds that live in small flocks of 6–12 birds.

Looking After the Chicks

Macaws make nests in holes near the top of trees. Usually macaws lay two eggs. The chicks are blind and featherless when they hatch. The parents feed and care for them for four months before they are able to fly and leave the nest.

Keeping Watch

When macaws feed in large groups, there are always one or two macaws to keep watch. This protects them from their predators, such as jaguars and harpy eagles.

Bright plumage provides excellent camouflage in trees

AMAZING COLORFUL BIRD FACTS!

● Young acorn woodpeckers stay with their parents for several years and help them raise more young.

● The green-winged macaw is one of the largest parrots, measuring up to 36 in. (90 cm) tall.

● The aracari nests in old woodpecker holes.

● When feeding, lorikeets often hang upside down so they can get a better grip on the tree branch.

● The green-winged macaw has a strong, hooked beak for eating fruit, seeds, and nuts.

● When sleeping, a toucan turns its head so its long bill rests on its back. Then, it folds its tail neatly over its beak.

15

Water Birds

Greater Flamingoes

There are about 900 species of birds that have adapted to a wide range of watery habitats. Some have webbed feet for swimming. Others have long legs and necks for wading in shallow water. Many have long, sharp beaks, which they use to stab their **prey**, the animals they hunt.

Atlantic Puffin

The **greater flamingo** has a **wingspan** of 55 in. (140 cm) and is 42 in. (107 cm) tall. It has a specially adapted bill that it uses to capture and filter its food from the water. The parents take turns incubating a single egg.

The **Atlantic puffin** lives at sea and is an excellent swimmer. It can dive underwater up to 200 ft. (61 m) deep in search of sand eels, its main food. It digs burrows in cliff tops.

American Bittern

The **American bittern** has brown and cream-colored striped feathers, which provide excellent camouflage. To avoid being seen, the bittern stands still with its bill pointed skyward. In this position, it sways slowly from side to side to imitate swaying reeds.

Mandarin Ducks

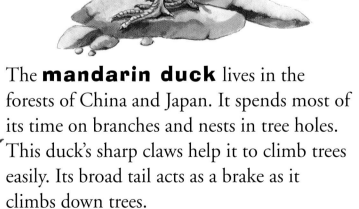

The **brown booby** makes dives from the air into the water from 100 ft. (30 m) to grab fish in its long beak. Its nostrils are completely sealed to stop water from being forced in when it dives. On land, the brown booby has to breathe through its mouth.

Brown Boobies

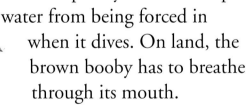

The **mandarin duck** lives in the forests of China and Japan. It spends most of its time on branches and nests in tree holes. This duck's sharp claws help it to climb trees easily. Its broad tail acts as a brake as it climbs down trees.

Brown Pelican

The brown pelican can be found along the coasts of North and South America, Central America, and the Caribbean. It is 5 ft. (1.5 m) long and has a heavy body and long neck. Large, webbed feet push the pelican through the water and help it steer when it dives in. The pelican's distinguishing feature is its large throat pouch.

Diving for Food

Unlike other species of pelicans that sit on the water to fish for food, the brown pelican dives from the air while gliding over the water. Once it sees a school of fish, it flies about 12 ft. (3.7 m) upward, folds back its wings, then dives into the water for the catch.

Pelican Parents

Both male and female adults incubate the eggs. The parents **regurgitate**, or throw up, finely chewed fish for the baby pelicans' first ten days. Once their eyes are open, the chicks take food from their parents' beaks.

Cushioned Dive

The pelican has air sacs beneath its skin. These sacs cushion the pelican from the impact of hitting the water when it dives. It also has small nostrils to help keep water from being forced in.

Flying

The brown pelican's bones are more hollow, or have more air inside them, than other birds' bones. This makes this large bird lighter and helps it to fly.

The pelican uses its pouch to scoop up fish

Throat Pouch

The pelican uses its bill and throat pouch like a net to scoop up fish and water. It strains out water from the sides of its bill, tips back its head, then swallows the fish. The pouch is also used for drinking freshwater.

Changing Colors

Like many water birds, the pelican's outer feathers are water repellent. The pelican is usually silver-gray on its back, black on its body, and white on its head and neck. Its neck turns brown and its head turns yellow in the breeding season.

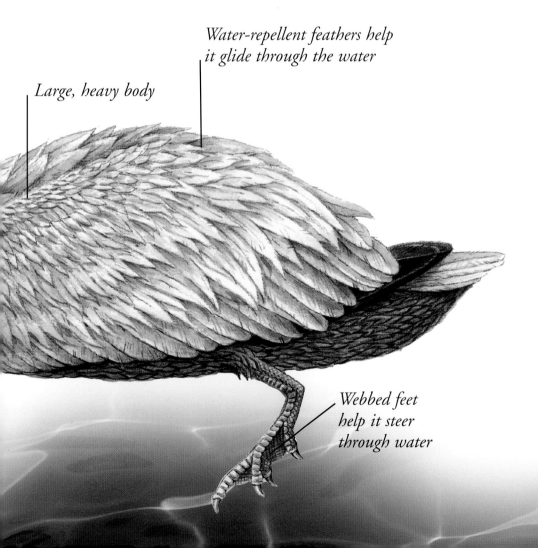

Water-repellent feathers help it glide through the water

Large, heavy body

Webbed feet help it steer through water

AMAZING WATER BIRD FACTS!

- Most water birds have **water-repellent** feathers.

- The pink flamingo's color comes from chemicals called *carotenoids*, contained in the algae and tiny creatures they eat.

- The brown pelican's throat pouch can hold about 3 gal. (11 l) of water and fish.

- Brown pelicans make chirping noises as chicks, but are voiceless as adults.

- The brown pelican has large, webbed feet for swimming and for steering when underwater.

- The female mandarin duck calls from the ground to her newly-hatched chicks in the trees. The chicks crawl out from the tree hole, fall to the ground unhurt, then follow the mother to find food.

Birds of Prey

Vultures, eagles, and owls are skilled hunters and **scavengers**. They have sharp, hooked beaks for tearing up live prey and **carcasses**, the bodies of dead animals. Birds of prey have long toes and sharp **talons**, or claws, to grab their prey. Their excellent eyesight helps them see their prey from a distance.

Bald Eagle

The **bald eagle** has a wingspan of 8 ft. (2.4 m), a hooked beak, and sharp, curved talons. It has one long, backward-pointing talon, which helps the eagle hold its prey. It helps clean up the environment by eating **carrion**, or dead-animal matter.

The **peregrine falcon** is one of the world's fastest birds. It uses its speed to hunt prey while it is flying. When it folds back its wings, the falcon can dive at speeds of 100–150 mph (160–240 km/h) toward its prey.

Peregrine Falcon

The **snowy owl** has extra-thick white feathers to keep it warm in the Arctic tundra. The owl's feathers extend to its toes to keep its legs warm. The feathers even cover part of its beak. This plumage also provides excellent camouflage in the snow.

The **crested caracara** is so-named because of the crest on the back of its head. It spends most of its time on the ground, but often flies over grasslands looking for carrion to feed on. The caracara has long legs that it uses to walk through long grass.

Snowy Owl

Crested Caracara

The **common poorwill** is named for its call, which sounds like "poor-will." It is one of the few birds known to **hibernate** in winter. This allows it to go without food for long periods of time when food is scarce. At other times, it hunts for insects at night.

Common Poorwill

Great Horned Owl

The great horned owl is found in North, Central, and South America. It lives in a variety of habitats, including forest, **scrubland**, and mountains. It nests in trees, in caves, on the ledges of cliffs, and even on the ground. At 24 in. (60 cm) in length, it is one of the largest American owls. Above its yellow eyes, the great horned owl has crests of feathers that look like horns.

Nighttime Hunter

The great horned owl is a skillful nighttime hunter. It has a flexible neck so its head can be turned 270°—almost all the way around—while its body stays still. This helps it hear the slightest sounds, such as a mouse moving through the grass.

Owl Eyes

The great horned owl's eyes are much larger than any other bird's. This means that its eyes gather as much light as possible at night. Owls are able to judge distances and the size of prey. Their vision is 100 times more powerful than a human being's vision.

On the Lookout

The great horned owl keeps watch from trees or posts, looking for prey.

Beaks and Claws

The great horned owl has a sharp, hooked beak for tearing flesh, and powerful talons for grabbing prey.

Eating Habits

Once a day, the owl regurgitates a pellet-like object that contains the fur and bones of prey that it cannot digest.

Feathers look like horns

Powerful Wings

Large eyes face forward and help the owl judge distances

The great horned owl has large, powerful wings that are covered in soft feathers. This helps it to glide down silently, surprising its prey.

Sharp, powerful talons are used to grasp prey

AMAZING BIRDS OF PREY FACTS!

● Birds of prey are able to see much farther than human beings can see, and have excellent hearing.

● The smallest bird of prey is the pygmy falcon, weighing less than a pencil.

● The largest bird of prey is the Martial eagle, which weighs 11 lbs. (5 kg) and has a wingspan of 7 ft. (2 m).

● The great horned owl has eyes in the front of its head to help it judge distances.

● The bald eagle is not really bald—it has a white head. The word "bald" comes from *balde*, an Old English word meaning "white."

● The bald eagle can actually swim! It uses an overhand motion of its wings that resembles the butterfly stroke.

Small Birds

There are about 900 species of hummingbirds, swifts, and finches. Hummingbirds and swifts have a special wing structure, which makes these birds flexible when they fly. Their quick twists and turns make them look like acrobats in the air. Small birds are very active and fly fast. They are constantly on the move.

Common Swifts

The **common swift** has a short, forked tail, long body, and long, pointed wings. It spends most of its time in the air, landing only to build its nest and feed its young. Its small beak can open wide and trap insects while it flies.

Crossbill

The **crossbill** is a medium-sized, stocky finch with a fairly large head. The upper and lower parts of its beak are crossed. This helps it remove seeds, its only food, from the cones of pine and spruce trees.

Sword-Billed Hummingbird

The **sword-billed hummingbird** has a 5-in. (12.5-cm) long beak, which is as long as its head and body combined. It uses its beak to probe deep down into tube-shaped flowers. This allows it to suck nectar that birds with shorter beaks cannot reach.

Zebra Finch

The **house sparrow** is also known as the *English sparrow*. Although its short beak is like that of a seed-eater, this sparrow has adapted to feed on worms, fruit, and even scraps of human beings' food.

House Sparrows

The **zebra finch** has long, thin toes that are ideal for holding onto grasses and twigs while it is feeding on seeds. It keeps seeds in a special groove in its short, pointed beak. This holds the seeds in place while the bird crushes them.

Anna's Hummingbird

Anna's hummingbird lives mostly in the woodlands and scrublands of California. It can be found as far north as British Columbia or as far south as Arizona. It is found in areas where there are nectar-producing flowers. This hummingbird grows to just 3¾ in. (9.5 cm), including its beak. Its glossy feathers appear to change color as it moves in the sunlight.

Hummingbird Chicks

Anna's hummingbird breeds very early in spring. The male selects the nesting place and defends the territory. The female makes a small cup-shaped nest using plant material held together with spiders' webs. She lays two eggs and incubates them. The female looks after the chicks for about a month after they hatch. The male takes no role in rearing the chicks.

Flowers for Food

Nectar is found in flowers and is a high-energy food. Anna's hummingbird has a poor sense of smell, but is attracted to flowers by their shape and color.

Eating to Survive

Nectar is the
hummingbird's main food.
It must eat half its body
weight in nectar each day
to survive. It also feeds
on tiny insects and
the red gooseberry.

Long, thin bill

Forward and Backward

This bird has strong chest muscles and shoulder joints that can move in all directions. This means that it can fly forward, backward, sideways, up, and down!

Beak probes into flower for nectar

Little Helicopter

The hummingbird beats its wings in a figure-eight pattern. It can hover in the air much like a helicopter. When this hummingbird flies, its wings beat 60 times per second. Its wings can beat one million times without stopping!

Anna's hummingbird can hover in front of flowers while feeding

Hummingbirds are often smaller than the flowers they feed on

AMAZING SMALL BIRD FACTS!

- Many small birds have bright plumage.

- Hummingbirds are the only birds that can fly backward.

- The smallest bird in the world is the bee hummingbird. It is about the size of a penny. It would take 240 of them to weigh just one pound!

- A hummingbird's heart beats up to 1,200 times per minute!

- The Anna's hummingbird has a special groove in its tongue that allows nectar to roll down its throat.

- The Anna's hummingbird's feet are small and weak, and are useless for walking.

- Swifts spend so much time in the air, they can sleep while they are flying!

27

Glossary

bill The beak of a bird.

camouflage Colors and markings on an animal that help it to blend in with its surroundings. This makes it difficult for both prey and predators to see the animal.

carcass The body of a dead animal.

carrion The bodies or parts of dead animals.

endangered Refers to a species that has such a small population left that it is in danger of becoming extinct.

extinct Refers to a species that no longer exists.

flock A large gathering of birds.

habitat The area in which an animal normally lives and grows.

hibernate To sleep or become inactive during winter as a result of cold weather and lack of food.

incubate To sit on eggs in order to keep them warm.

nectar A sweet liquid found in various plants and flowers.

bill

camouflage

extinct

28

nocturnal Active mainly at night.

plumage The feathers of a bird.

predator An animal that hunts and eats other animals.

prey An animal that is hunted and eaten by other animals.

rain forest A tropical forest with an annual rainfall of at least 100 in. (254 cm).

regurgitate To bring partly digested food back into the mouth to feed young.

roost To rest or sleep.

plumage

scavenger An animal that searches for dead and decaying flesh on which to feed.

scrubland An area with straggly, stunted trees and bushes.

species A group of individuals having common characteristics.

talon A hooked claw.

water-repellent Refers to feathers that help prevent water from reaching the bird's skin.

wingspan The distance from wing tip to wing tip when the wings are outstretched.

wingspan

Index

30